Discover Islam

Edited by
Al-Jumuah staff

© Aljumuah Magazine for Editing & Pub, 2003
King Fahd National Library cataloging-in-Publication Data

Al-Jumuah Staff
Discover Islam. / Al-Jumuah Staff.-Riyadh, 2003..
P; ..cm

ISBN: 9960-9406-7-6
1-Islam   I-Title
210 dc   1426/5027

L.D. no. 1426/5027
ISBN: 9960-9406-7-5

Third Edition
1429H – 2008G

Table of Contents

بسم الله الرحمن الرحيم

Discover Islam
Edited by al-Jumuah Staff

Foreword

There is hardly any place on earth today where Islam is totally unknown. More and more people have become curious enough to find out something about this much publicized religion; more often than not, they have been pleasantly surprised.

Islam is the religion and way of life of about one fifth of the world's population. Muslims are of diverse nationalities, cultures and races, but their religion teaches that all humanity is essentially equal. Islam is generally misunderstood and misrepresented in contemporary Western societies; therefore, it is hoped that this booklet will help shed light on Islam and dispel many of the prevailing misconceptions.

With this objective in mind, *al-Jumuah Magazine* presents a brief overview of Islam, followed by answers to some of the most commonly asked questions by non-Muslims.

Islamic Beliefs

The Islamic creed did not begin with the prophethood of Muhammad (ﷺ)[1], nor was it invented by him. It is essentially the same message contained in previous divine scriptures and taught by all prophets of Allah. Islamic beliefs are eternal truths that neither change nor develop; it provides truths about Allah and His relationship with the visible and invisible aspects of the universe, about the reality of this life, man's role therein and what will become of him afterwards. The requirements, or "pillars", of the Islamic faith are: belief in Allah, in the angels created by Him, in His scriptures, in the prophets through whom His revelation was conveyed to humanity, in the eternal life after death and in Allah's perfect judgment and complete authority over human destiny.

Belief in Allah

Monotheism is the essence of Islam, and it emphasizes the Oneness of Allah. Muslims believe in One eternal and unique God. He is the Creator of all that exists, yet He cannot be compared to anything of His creation. Muslims acknowledge that Allah alone

---

[1] This symbol means, 'may Allah exalt his mention and render him safe from all evil.'

is divine, that He alone is the Creator and Sustainer of creation. He is all-knowing and all-powerful, completely just and merciful.

Allah is not part of His creation, nor is any of it a part of Him. The significance of exclusive divinity is that no one and nothing in existence is worthy to be worshipped except Allah, the Creator and Sustainer of all things. In Islam everything is built upon the Oneness of Allah. No act of worship has any meaning if the concept of monotheism is in any way compromised.

The proper name of God is "Allah". He is the same God known to Christians, Jews and to people of other monotheistic faiths. Allah sent a series of messages to mankind through appointed prophets and messengers. Quite a few of them are familiar to people of Judeo-Christian background, such as Adam, Noah, Abraham, Moses, Jesus and many others (ﷺ)[2].

Belief in the Angels

Muslims believe that Angels exist. No one knows their exact number except Him. They obey Him, fulfill His commands, and guard over the universe and the creatures that dwell within it. They carry out

---

[2] This symbol means, 'may Allah redner him safe from all evil' and is said after a Prophet or Messenger's name.

the orders of Allah, from administration, observation, guarding and protecting the universe as well as its creatures, all according to Allah's Will and Order. Allah has revealed to us the names of some of the angels; for example, Gabriel, who was given the task of revelation, Michael, who has been assigned the task of directing rain and vegetation. There is also the Angel of Death, who has been given the task of collecting the souls at their appointed times.

Belief in the Scriptures

Muslims also believe in the original scriptures revealed by Allah, such as the Scriptures of Abraham and Moses, the Torah, the Psalms of David and the Gospel of Jesus. The final revelation to humanity is the Qur'an, which was revealed to Prophet Muhammad (ﷺ). The Qur'an remains preserved and unchanged since the time of revelation in its original Arabic text. There is only one version of the Qur'an. It is recited and memorized by Muslims throughout the world. It contains the final message to humanity and legislation which both encompasses all spheres of human life and is also suited to all peoples and all times. Moreover, it contains numerous verses that speak of the universe, its components and phenomena - the earth, sun, moon, stars, mountains, wind, rivers and seas, plants, animals, as well as the successive stages of human embryonic development.

One of the miracles of the Qur'an, and evidence of its divine origins, is that nothing within it contradicts any established scientific fact.

Belief in the Messengers

A Muslim is required to believe that Allah chose the finest amongst humanity to be Messengers whom He sent to His creation with specific legislations: to worship and obey Him and to establish His religion and His Oneness. Allah, the Almighty, says:

❨And We did not send any Messenger before you [O Muhammad (ﷺ)] but We inspired him [saying]: none has the right to be worshipped but I (Allah), so worship Me (Alone and none else).❩ [21:25]

The last of the divinely appointed messengers was Prophet Muhammad (ﷺ). To him was conveyed the final and complete revelation from Allah. All the prophets preached the same basic message: the worship of Allah alone. In essence, they all preached *Islam*, which means willing, peaceful submission to Allah, the one true God; Creator of the universe.

The final prophet was sent by the Creator as a human model to be followed and obeyed. Prophet Muhammad (ﷺ) exemplified the principles laid down in the Qur'an, and true Muslims strive to follow his noble example. His biography has been recorded in minute detail and is easily accessible for study. There is a complete, authentically narrated documentation of his sayings and practices which is the second source of Islamic legislation. It is complementary to the Qur'an and supplements it with additional details and clarification of meanings. This record contains the prophetic traditions referred to as the *Sunnah*. Scholars have carefully and painstakingly scrutinized the reliability of the transmitters of these traditions, and only those whose narrators are found to be completely reliable and sound are accepted.

Belief in the Last Day

Muslims believe that the life of this world will come to an end. Allah says:

❨**Whatsoever is on it** (i.e. the earth) **will perish.**❩

[55:26]

The Day of Resurrection is the day when each individual will stand before Allah and be questioned about their deeds. The compensation for evil in the Hereafter is exact justice, while the compensation for good is much greater - comprehensive, multiple rewards and complete satisfaction and happiness.

People will be judged according to their degree of righteousness, and nothing else. Allah says:

❨Whoever brings a good deed shall have ten times the like thereof to his (or her) credit, and whoever brings an evil deed shall have only the recompense of the like thereof.❩ [6:160]

A person is rewarded for merely intending to do good, even if they do not follow up that intention with action. Prophet Muhammad (ﷺ) mentioned that Allah said:

"Whoever intends to perform a good deed but does not do it, Allah records it for them as one good deed. If one intends to do a good deed and does it, Allah records for them the like thereof ten times, up to seven hundred times, to many times. If one intends to do an evil deed, but does not do it, Allah records it for them as one good deed. If one intends to do an evil deed and does it, Allah records it only as one evil deed."

[Bukhari]

Belief in Predestination

Muslims believe in predestination, whether good or bad, which Allah has measured and ordained for all creatures according to His previous knowledge and as deemed suitable by His wisdom. Allah, the All-Knowing, knows everything that happened in the past, everything that is happening now and all that will happen in the future. Humankind has been given free will and the choice of whether or not to follow what Allah ordained. He has been given a mind with which he is able to reason and choose wisely.

The Requirements of Islam

The five "pillars" of Islam make up the framework of a Muslim's life, they are:

1. The 'Shahadah' or Declaration of Faith

To be a Muslim, one must believe in and pronounce words that mean, "*There is no deity worthy of being worshipped except Allah and Muhammad is His slave and messenger.*"[3] This declaration testifies that Allah exists, that He is unlike and superior to His creation and that none is worthy of worship but Him. It also testifies that He is the Creator and Proprietor of all that exists and Disposer of all affairs. Allah says in the Qur'an:

❨No doubt! Verily, to Allah belongs whosoever is in the heavens and whosoever is in the earth. And those that worship and invoke others besides Allah, in fact follow not these associated-gods; they follow only a conjecture and they invent only lies.❩ [10:66]

---

[3] The Arabic wording is: '*Laa ilaahah il'lal-laah Muhammad Rasool Allah.*'

The 'Shahadah' testifies that Muhammad is among the prophets who conveyed Allah's revelation to humankind. Allah says:

❨And We have not sent you (O Muhammad (ﷺ)) except to all of humankind, as a giver of glad tidings and a Warner, but most people know not.❩ [34:28]

In fact, it is stated in the Qur'an that Muhammad (ﷺ) is the last of Allah's messengers. Allah says:

❨Muhammad is not the father of any man among you, but he is the Messenger of Allah and the last of the Prophets.❩ [33:40]

The Qur'an also confirms that Muhammad's teachings are infallible and conveyed from Allah. Allah says:

❨Nor does he speak of (his own) desire. It is only an Inspiration that is inspired.❩ [53:3-4]

Thus, the Qur'an, and Sunnah of the final prophet, are the basis of the religion, and they define every aspect of the Islamic way of life.

2. The 'Salah', or Formal Obligatory Prayer

Prayer was practiced in some form throughout history by all prophets and their followers as an indispensable part of Allah's religion. Islam, the final message to humanity, considers prayer essential. A Muslim is required to pray five times daily within specified intervals, as taught by the Prophet (ﷺ). These prayers are obligatory, and form a direct bond between the worshipper and his Creator. Islam does not call upon Muslims to merely perform this act of worship; rather; it wants of them to purify their souls. Allah (ﷻ) says, regarding Prayer:

❴Indeed the prayer prevents [you] from licentiousness and [other] sins.❵ [29:45]

3. 'Zakah' or Obligatory Annual Charity

The word "Zakah" means purification and growth. An important principle of Islam is that all things belong to Allah. Muslims are enjoined to earn and spend their wealth in ways that are acceptable to Allah. The divinely ordained system of *Zakah* is the right of Allah within His dominion. It is neither a charity nor a tax, but an obligation due from Muslims who possess wealth in excess of their basic needs. Thus, the difference between *Zakah* and tax is that a Muslim pays *Zakah* willfully and on their own accord; they are the ones who supervise its payment.

Zakah is only due when a person has the minimum required amount, which varies with the type of wealth.

Zakah cleanses a Muslim of greed, selfishness, base covetousness, and the love of this temporal world. Allah (﷾) says:

❨And whosoever is saved from his own covetousness, such are they who will be the successful.❩ [59:9]

It is the ideal way to meet the needs of the poorer sections of society without causing hardship to the wealthy.

4. 'Siyam' or Fasting

Allah has enjoined fasting upon the Muslims as He enjoined it upon previous nations. He, the Exalted, says:

❨O you who believe! Fasting has been prescribed for you as it was prescribed for those before you, that you may become the pious.❩

[2:183]

Islamic fasting, which involves abstinence from eating, drinking, sexual intercourse and all prohibited habits such as smoking, is observed throughout the daylight hours of the lunar month of

Ramadhan. When done in obedience to God's command, fasting teaches believers patience and self-control, as well as reminding them of their responsibility toward the millions of human beings who lack provisions or are victims of their unjust distribution. The month of fasting is accompanied by increased efforts toward good manners and righteous deeds, along with additional worship at night. Fasting is not a retreat from life; rather, it is a supplement to the Muslim's ordinary activities.

5. 'Hajj' or Pilgrimage

Hajj, the annual pilgrimage to Makkah (in Saudi Arabia), is a once-in-a-lifetime obligation for those who are physically and financially able to perform it. Allah says:

❨Pilgrimage to the House (i.e. the Ka'bah) is incumbent upon men for the sake of Allah, (upon) everyone who is able to undertake the journey to it.❩ [3:97]

Nevertheless, millions of Muslims journey to Makkah each year from every corner of the globe, providing a unique opportunity for people of various nations to meet one another as guests of Allah. Hajj is an expression of pure faith and total submission to His command, and the pilgrim performs rites of unqualified obedience, seeking nothing but the acceptance of their efforts and forgiveness of their past sins. A person who has completed the Hajj returns with a fresh outlook on life, a purified soul and blessings from Allah.

Muhammad the Messenger of Allah (ﷺ)

Introduction

It all began in the year 610 C.E.[4], with a few brave individuals differing in tribe, status, and gender, secretly winding through the alleys of *Makkah* to meet the man known as *Al-Ameen* (i.e. the trustworthy). One by one they went, like stealthy shadows in the moonlight, hoping not to be noticed and reported to powerful city leaders. They were prepared to sacrifice it all – their cultures, families, even their own lives – for the sake of worshipping One True God.

Al-Ameen had called them to cast aside the pagan religion of their forefathers, and to embrace pure monotheism. The 40-year-old man, whose name was Muhammad, (ﷺ), claimed that Allah saw all people, men and women, free and enslaved, as equal: A message which would, in two short decades, bring peace to the war-torn Arabian Peninsula and beyond; a message forbidding tribal feudalism and corruption by any leader; a message that came to be known as "Islam," calling for devotion and submission to God alone.

---

[4] Common Era or Christian Era, in preference to A.D. (Anno Domini) meaning 'the year of the Lord'.

Who was he?

Muhammad (ﷺ) was a man of noble descent. He was a paradigm of excellent manners. Allah, the Exalted, praised him saying:

❴And verily, you (O Muhammad ﷺ) are on an exalted (standard of) character.❵ [68:4]

His enemies attested to his excellent manners. Abu Jahl, who was one of the harshest enemies of Islam, said: 'O Muhammad! I do not say that you are a liar! I only deny what you brought and what you call people to.'

Some of his Companions described his manners saying:

'He was never rough. He never raised his voice in public or used foul language. He did not repay evil with evil; rather, he forgave and pardoned. He did not raise his hand to hit a servant or woman. He would not become angry if he was wronged, nor would he avenge himself. He only became angry when people transgressed the limits and boundaries of Allah; in that case he avenged. The Prophet (ﷺ) was not given a choice between two matters, except that he chose the easier of the two, as long as it was not a sinful act. If that act was a sinful act, he would be the farthest from it.

When he entered his home he was a normal individual, he would clean his clothes, milk his sheep, and serve himself.'

Thomas Carlyle, the famous Scottish writer, attested to this. He said in his book 'Heroes, Hero-Worship, and the Heroic in History':

'But, from an early age, he had been remarked as a thoughtful man. His companions named him "*Al Amin*, The Faithful." A man of truth and fidelity; true in what he did, in what he spoke and thought. They noted that he always meant something. A man rather taciturn in speech; silent when there was nothing to be said; but pertinent, wise, sincere, when he did speak; always throwing light on the matter. This is the only sort of speech worth speaking! Through life we find him to have been regarded as an altogether solid, brotherly, genuine man. A serious, sincere character; yet amiable, cordial, companionable, jocose even - a good laugh in him withal: there are men whose laugh is as untrue as anything about them; who cannot laugh. A spontaneous, passionate, yet just, true-meaning man! Full of wild faculty, fire and light; of wild worth, all uncultured; working out his life - takes in the depth of the Desert there.'

'They called him a prophet, you say? Why, he stood there face to face with them, here, not enshrined in any mystery, visibly clouting his own cloak, cobbling his own shoes, fighting, counseling ordering in the midst of them. They must have seen what kind of a man he was, let him be called what ye like. No emperor with his tiaras was obeyed as this man in a cloak of his own clouting. During three and twenty years of rough, actual trial, I find something of a veritable hero necessary for that of itself.'

If we say the physical appearance of a person influences their personality, as do sociologists, the Prophet (ﷺ) was the most beautiful of people as his companions, who saw him, informed us. The Prophet (ﷺ) was of a slightly above-average height. Amazingly, in gatherings, he would appear taller than those actually taller than him - until the people dispersed. In complexion, he was white with a rosy tinge; pale, but not excessively so. His hair was jet black and wavy, but stopped short of curling, and was kept between his earlobes and shoulders. Sometimes he would part his hair at the middle. Other times, he would wear it braided. The Prophet (ﷺ) had the physique of a powerful man. He had a broad upper-back and shoulders, between which was the Seal of Prophet-hood. He had long muscular limbs, large joints and a wide girth. His lean stomach never protruded out past the profile of his chest. His face was radiant, **"as if the sun were following its course across and**

shining from his face," His shoulders were broad; he was of medium height, neither too tall nor short. He was pleasant looking and majestic; people were full of awe when they saw him for the first time, and knew that his face was not one of a liar.

Prophecies

Prophet Jesus (عليه السلام) foretold the coming of another Prophet, whose name would be 'Periqlytos' or 'Paraclete' or 'Paracalon' and who (that is, whose teaching) would last forever, **'I will pray the Father, and He shall give you another Comforter** (Periqlytos)**, that he may abide with you forever.'** [John 14, 16].

The word periqlytos means 'illustrious, 'renowned' and 'praiseworthy' and this is exactly what the name 'Ahmed' means. It is confirmed in the Qur'an that the Prophet Jesus did prophesize that a Prophet named 'Ahmed' would come after him.

Allah, the Exalted, says:

❨**And remember when Jesus the son of Mary, said: "O Children of Israel! I am the Messenger of Allah unto you, confirming the Torah which came before me, and giving glad tidings of a**

Messenger to come after me, whose name shall be Ahmed.⟫ [61:6]

The Jews sent priests to John, the Baptist, to find out who he was. 'He confessed, "I am not the Christ." And they asked him, ''What then? Are you Elijah?" And He said: "I am not." ''Are you that *Prophet*?" They insisted. And he answered, "No"… And then they said to him: "Why do you baptize then, if you are not the Christ, nor Elijah, nor that *Prophet*?" (John 1:20-25).

'That Prophet' is not Jesus, but Muhammad (ﷺ) because John the Baptist continued preaching and baptizing and foretelling the coming of that *Prophet* during the life-time of Jesus.

What they said about Muhammad (ﷺ)

Alphonse de Lamartine said: 'Never has a man set for himself, voluntarily or involuntarily, a more sublime aim, since this aim was superhuman; to subvert superstitions which had been imposed between man and his Creator, to render God unto man and man unto God; to restore the rational and sacred idea of divinity amidst the chaos of the material and disfigured gods of idolatry, then existing. Never has a man undertaken a work so far beyond human power with so feeble means, for he (Muhammad) had in the conception as well as in the execution of such a great design, no other instrument than himself and no other aid except a handful of men living in a corner of the desert. Finally, never has a man accomplished such a huge and lasting revolution in the world, because. in less than two centuries after its appearance, Islam, in faith and in arms, reigned over the whole of Arabia, and conquered, in God's name, Persia Khorasan, Transoxania, Western India, Syria, Egypt, Abyssinia, all the known continent of Northern Africa, numerous islands of the Mediterranean Sea, Spain, and part of Gaul. "If greatness of purpose, smallness of means, and astonishing results are the three criteria of a human genius, who could dare compare any great man in history with Muhammad."'[5]

George Bernard Shaw said: 'I have always held the religion of Muhammad in high estimation because of its wonderful vitality. It is the only religion which appears to possess that assimilating capability to the changing phases of existence which make itself appeal to every age - I have prophesized about the faith of Muhammad that it would be acceptable tomorrow as it is beginning to

---

[5] Alphonse de LaMartaine in 'Histoire de la Turquie,' Paris, 1854.

be acceptable to the Europe of today. Medieval ecclesiastics, either through ignorance or bigotry, painted Mohammedanism in the darkest colors. They were, in fact, trained to hate both the man Muhammad and his religion. To them, Muhammad was an anti-Christ. I have studied him, the wonderful man, and in my opinion, far from being an anti-Christ, he must be called the Savior of humanity - '[6]

The German Poet, Wolfgang Göthe[7], said: 'I looked into history for a human paradigm and found it to be in Muhammad (ﷺ).'

---

[6] 'The Genuine Islam,' Vol. 1, No. 8, 1936.

[7] A German writer and scientist: Master of poetry, drama, and the novel, he also conducted scientific research in various fields, notably botany, and held several governmental positions.

QUESTIONS AND ANSWERS

Creedal Issues

1) Who is Allah? Do Muslims worship a different God?

Some people believe that Muslims worship a God that is different from the one worshipped by Christians and Jews. This might be due to the fact that Muslims often refer to God as *"Allah"*. This concept is false, since "Allah" is simply the Arabic word for the One true "God" Who created the universe and all humanity. Let there be no doubt - Muslims worship the God of Noah, Abraham, Moses, David and Jesus (ﷺ). However, it is certainly true that Jews, Christians and Muslims all have different concepts of Almighty God. For example, Muslims - like Jews - reject the Christian beliefs of the Trinity and the Divine Incarnation. This, however, does not mean that each of these three religions worships a different God - because, as we have already said, there is only One True God. Judaism, Christianity and Islam all claim to be "Abrahamic Faiths", and all of them are also classified as "monotheistic." However, Islam teaches that other religions have, in one way or another, distorted and nullified a pure and proper belief in Almighty God by neglecting His true teachings and mixing them with man-made ideas. Islam calls upon people to return to the one true God and to worship and obey Him alone. Islam teaches that God should be approached without intermediaries. That is because the merciful all-knowing God is completely in control of everything that exists and that He can bestow His grace and mercy on His creatures as He pleases; therefore no intercession, atonement or incarnation is necessary.

Arabic speaking people of all religions refer to God as "Allah". For example, if you pick up an Arabic translation of the Christian Bible you will see the word *"Allah"* where "God" is used in English. Therefore, Allah is not the god of only the Muslims, but the same God worshipped by all monotheistic faiths. This idea that "Allah" is different from "God" is illogical since it is tantamount to saying that the French worship a different "god" because they use the word "Dieu", that Spaniards worship a different "god" because they say "Dios" or that the Hebrews worshipped a different "god" because they called Him "Yahweh"!

The Qur'an, which is the divine scripture of Muslims, was revealed in the Arabic language, so Muslims use the word "Allah" for "God", even when they are speaking other languages. A more literal translation of "Allah" into English might be "the one-and-only God" or "the one true God".

It should be clearly understood that what Islam is primarily concerned with is correcting humankind's concept of Almighty God. What people are ultimately going to be held accountable for at the end of Day of Judgment is not whether they preferred the word "Allah" or the word "God", but what their concept of Him is. The true concept of God is clarified only within the message revealed by Him. The last message sent by God, or Allah, is the Qur'an.

2) The Qur'an uses the word 'We' when quoting Allah. Does that mean that Muslims believe in more than one God?

Islam adheres to uncompromising monotheism. It teaches that God is One and indivisible. In the Qur'an, God often refers to Himself as "We". But it does not mean that there is more than one God. The reference of God to Himself as "We" in many Qur'anic verses is necessarily understood in the Arabic language to denote power and grandeur, as opposed to the more intimate singular form, "I", used in specific instances.

In some languages there are two types of plural form. One is related to quantity and used to refer to two or more persons, places or things. The other kind of plural is one of majesty, power and distinction. For example, in proper English, the Queen of England refers to herself as 'we'. This is known as the 'royal plural'. Rajeev Gandhi, the ex-Prime Minister of India used to say in Hindi, *"Hum dekhna chahte hain"*. "We want to see." *'Hum'* means 'we', which is again a royal plural in Hindi language. Similarly, when God refers to Himself in the Qur'an, He sometimes uses the Arabic word *'nahnu'*, meaning 'We'. It does not indicate a plurality of number but the plurality of power and majesty.

The oneness of God is stressed throughout the Qur'an. A clear example is in this short chapter:

❨**Say: He is Allah [who is] One; Allah is He on Whom all depend. He neither begets nor is born, nor is there to Him any equivalent.**❩ [112:1-4]

3) **The Qur'an says that Allah is merciful and that He gives severe punishment. So is He forgiving or is He vengeful?**

The Qur'an mentions many times that God is the Most Merciful. In fact, all except one of the 114 chapters of the Qur'an begin with *Bismillaahir-Rahmaanir-Raheem*, which means, "I begin with the name of God, the Entirely Merciful and the Especially Merciful". These two descriptions of God are sometimes translated as "The Compassionate, the Merciful"; however in Arabic grammar, both names are an intensive form of the word "merciful". *Rahmaan* means merciful to all creation, and justice is part of this mercy. *Raheem* means merciful especially to the believers and forgiveness is part of this mercy. A complimentary and comprehensive meaning is intended by the use of both of them together. In addition, Allah speaks of His forgiveness throughout the Qur'an. In fact, God's mercy and forgiveness have been mentioned together more than 70 times in the Qur'an. Allah repeatedly reminds us saying:

❰And Allah is Forgiving and Merciful❱

But He also gives severe punishment to those who deserve it. Allah told Prophet Muhammad (ﷺ):

❰Inform My slaves that it is I Who am the Forgiving, the Merciful, and that it is My punishment which is the [most] painful punishment.❱ [15:49-50]

Allah is just, and His justice necessitates that He reward those who obey and serve Him and punish those who disobey and rebel against Him. If Allah did not punish the sinful, wicked and evil people who deserve to be punished, it would not be justice. When punishment for wrongdoing is certain, it serves to deter potential offenders. In contrast, if Allah forgave everyone and punished no one, there would be no reason for legislation, ethics or even morality. Life on earth would be chaotic and nothing short of anarchy. True justice, with its true rewards and just penalties can only be found with Allah, and that is what He has promised in the Qur'an:

《We shall place the scales of justice for the Day of Judgment, so no soul will be dealt with unjustly at all. And if there is [even] the weight of a mustard seed, We will bring it forth. And sufficient are We to take account.》 [21:47]

Allah forgives all those who repent and correct themselves at any stage in their lives, and He has invited all people to His abundant forgiveness and mercy:

《Say: 'O My slaves who have transgressed against their souls! Despair not of the mercy of Allah. Indeed, Allah forgives all sins. Indeed, it is He who is the Forgiving, the Merciful. And return [in repentance] to your Lord and submit to Him before the punishment comes upon you; then you will not be helped. And follow the best of what was revealed to you from your Lord before the punishment comes upon you suddenly, while you do not perceive.》 [39:53-5]

4) Some believe that Muslims worship Muhammad. Is this true?

Muslims do not worship Muhammad (ﷺ) in any way. We believe that he was the last messenger sent by Allah and like all His other prophets and messengers, he was a human being. However, some people mistakenly assume that Muslims worship Muhammad and this is one of the reasons that Muslims were erroneously called "*Mohammedans*".

Muhammad, like Jesus, never claimed divine status. He called people to worship Almighty Allah alone, and he continually emphasized his humanity. In order to prevent his deification, Prophet Muhammad (ﷺ) always said to refer to him as "*Allah's slave and messenger*". He (ﷺ) said:

'Do not adulate me as the Christians adulated Jesus son of Mary. I am Allah's slave and messenger.' (Bukhari)

Muhammad was chosen to be Allah's final messenger and to communicate His message to us, not only in words, but also as a living example of its practical application. Muslims love and respect him because of his impeccable and upright moral character and because he conveyed the truth from Allah - which is the pure monotheism of Islam.

Muslims strive to follow the great example of Prophet Muhammad (ﷺ) but do not worship him in any way. Islam teaches Muslims to respect all of Allah's prophets and messengers. However, respecting and loving them does not mean worshipping them. Muslims know that all worship and prayer must be directed to Allah alone.

In fact, the worship of Muhammad - or anyone else – along with, or instead of, Almighty Allah is considered an unpardonable sin in Islam. Even if a person claims to be Muslim but worships or prays to anything other than God, it invalidates one's claim to Islam. The *Declaration of Faith* makes it clear that Muslims must worship Allah alone.

5) Is Islam fatalistic?

Most Muslims find it rather odd that their religion, which strikes a remarkable balance between faith and deeds, are sometimes accused of being "fatalistic". Perhaps this misconception came about because Muslims are known to say "*All praise is due to Allah*" whenever anything good or bad happens. This is because Muslims know that everything comes from God, the Creator of the universe, and occurs by His will. Thus, a Muslim worries less about material matters and views earthly life in a proper perspective. A true Muslim relies completely on Allah and knows that whatever happens is always for the best, whether one recognizes it or not, so one graciously accepts whatever cannot be changed.

This does not mean that Muslims should simply await destiny and take no action in life. On the contrary, Islam demands action and effort to change every undesirable situation. To be more precise, action is a required part of one's faith. If human beings did not have the ability to act, it would be unjust for Allah to expect them to do and to avoid certain things. Far from being "fatalistic", Islam teaches that man's main obligation in life is to act and exert effort in obedience to God.

Islam teaches that human beings should take positive action in this life and supplement it with prayer. Some people are lazy and careless and then blame the negative result on destiny or fate. Some even say that, if Allah had willed, they would not have sinned or committed crimes. All of these arguments are completely erroneous, because Allah has taught us how to live and has ordered us to always do what is right. Allah has not ordered us to do anything that we are unable to do or prohibited anything that we cannot avoid, because His justice is complete and perfect. Each individual is held responsible within the limits of their ability and not beyond it.

6) How can you confirm the existence of Life after Death?

The Qur'an teaches that the present life is a trial in preparation for the next realm of our existence. A day will come when the whole universe will be destroyed and recreated, and the dead will be resurrected to stand in judgment before Allah.

❨On the Day when the earth will be changed to another earth and so will be the heavens and they (all creatures) will appear before Allah, the One, the Irresistible.❩ [14:48]

The Day of Resurrection will be the beginning of another life, one that will be eternal. It is then that every person will be fully compensated by Allah for his or her good and evil deeds.

The explanation that the Qur'an gives about the necessity of life after death is exactly what the moral consciousness of man demands. If there were no life after death, the very belief in Allah would become meaningless, or even if one believed in Him, it would then be an unjust and indifferent deity, having once created man and no longer being concerned with his fate. Surely, Allah is just. He will punish the tyrants, whose crimes are beyond count - having killed hundreds of innocent people, created great corruption in society, enslaved numerous persons to serve their own whims, and so on. Because one has a short life span in this world and since numerous individuals are affected by one's actions, adequate punishments and rewards are not possible in this life. The Qur'an very emphatically states that the Day of Judgment will come and that Allah will decide the fate of each soul.

Each and every human being longs for justice. Even if one does not uphold it for others they want justice for themselves. For example, tyrants and oppressors who are intoxicated by power and influence and inflict pain and suffering on others will object vehemently if any injustice is done to them. The reason such people become insensitive to the suffering of others is that they feel that power and influence prevents others from doing injustice to them.

Any person who has suffered injustice, irrespective of financial or social status, almost certainly wants its perpetrator to be punished. Though a large number of criminals are punished, many of them get off lightly or even scot-free. They may continue to lead pleasant, even luxurious lives and enjoy a peaceful existence. Allah may not punish a criminal in this world but He will surely hold him accountable on the Day of Judgment and punish him.

It is true that a wrongdoer may receive part of the justice that is due to him in this world, but it will remain incomplete. The same is true of someone who deserves great reward and repayment - who has done much good, helped or taught many people, saved lives, suffered to uphold truth or patiently endured much hardship or injustice. No earthly compensation is adequate for such relentless courage and effort. These types of deeds can only be repaid in full in an eternal life where every individual affected by one's actions will testify for or against that person, and where one's innermost thoughts and intentions, known only to Allah, will be exposed and judged precisely and perfectly.

Belief in the Hereafter is completely logical. Allah has made certain things pleasing and desirable to us in this worldly life, such as justice, although it is usually unattainable. Though a person may obtain a good portion of earthly pleasures and many of his objectives, one remains convinced that the world is unjust. Now, why would the Creator implant in us the love for something we may not experience? The answer is that this life is only one portion of our existence and the Hereafter is the necessary conclusion which balances everything out. Whatever is missing here will be found there; and similarly, whatever is gained unlawfully here will result in deprivation there. That is the perfect and absolute justice Allah has promised.

Finally, Allah is able to create and re-create as He wills. He creates whatever He wills, however He wills, whenever He wills. Allah, the Exalted, says:

❨As We began the first creation, We will repeat it. [That is] a promise binding upon Us. Indeed, We shall do it.❩ [21:104]

The Qur'an and other Scriptures

7) Is it true that Muhammad (ﷺ) wrote the Qur'an or copied from the Bible?

In addressing this misconception, it is interesting to note that no other religious scripture claims to be totally the direct word of God as clearly and as often as the Qur'an. Allah says:

❰Do they not reflect upon the Qur'an? Had it been from [any] other than Allah, they would have found within it much contradiction.❱ [4:82]

At the time the Qur'an was revealed, the Arabs recognized that the language of the Qur'an was unique and distinctly different from the language spoken by Prophet Muhammad (ﷺ) and his people. This, in spite of the fact that the Arabs of that time were known for their skill in poetry and mastery of the Arabic language. Moreover, Muhammad (ﷺ) was known to be an unlettered man. The Qur'an mentions that Muhammad (ﷺ) did not read and write, so if this was false, certainly his contemporaries would have protested and exposed him. However, there are no reports of this. Without doubt there were people who rejected Muhammad's message, just like the message of other prophets were rejected, but none denied it for this reason.

It is also interesting to note that even though the Qur'an is not poetry, the Arabs were much less inclined to poetry after it was revealed. It can be said that the Qur'an is the piece of Arabic literature *par excellence* - and Muhammad's enemies, realized that as much as they tried, they could not outdo or even equal it.

It is not difficult to prove that Muhammad (ﷺ) did not possess the knowledge that is expounded and detailed in the Qur'an, such as the accurate knowledge of historical events, previous prophets and natural phenomena. The Qur'an mentions in several places that Muhammad (ﷺ) and his people did not know these things. Allah says:

❨**This is of the news of the Unseen which We reveal unto you; neither you nor your people knew it before this. So be patient. Surely, the (good) end is for the pious.**❩ [11:49]

Suffice it to say that not only is the Qur'an the most memorized and well preserved scripture on earth, it is also unequaled in its eloquence, spiritual impact, clarity of message and purity of its truth.

Furthermore, the Qur'an recounts several instances where Prophet Muhammad (ﷺ) was criticized and corrected by Allah for his unintentional human errors. Had he been the author of the Qur'an he would not have included these rebukes in the Qur'an. For example, the Prophet (ﷺ) was once deeply and earnestly engaged in attempting to invite one of the pagan leaders to Islam when he was interrupted by a blind man who had come to him for information and to learn the Qur'an. The Prophet (ﷺ) naturally disliked the interruption because he was hopeful of affecting the influential leader's heart toward Islam. He frowned and turned away, a gesture that went unnoticed by the blind man. No sooner had the Prophet (ﷺ) finished talking to the leader than he received the following revelation which he conveyed to his people without the least bit of hesitation:

❴He [i.e. the Prophet] **frowned and turned away, because there came to him the blind man. But what would make you perceive** [O Muhammad] **that perhaps he might be purified or be reminded, and the reminder would benefit him?**❵ [80:1-4]

This incident reflects the highest degree of sincerity on the part of the Prophet (ﷺ) regarding the revelation that was revealed to him. These verses provide substantial proof that the Prophet (ﷺ) was not the author of the Qur'an, nor was he the founder of Islam.

Some Christian critics often claim that Muhammad (ﷺ) was not himself the author of the Qur'an but that he learned, copied or adapted it from Jewish and Christian scriptures. In reality, however, Prophet Muhammad's contacts with the Jewish and Christian scholars were extremely limited. Historical records available show that he made only three trips outside Makkah before his prophethood: At the age of nine he accompanied his mother to Madinah. Before the age of twelve, he accompanied his uncle on a business trip to Syria. And before his marriage, at the age of 25, he led Khadijah's caravan to Syria. The most prominent Christian known to him was an old blind man named Waraqah bin Nawfal, who was a relative of his wife Khadijah. He was a convert to Christianity and well-versed in the Gospels. The Prophet (ﷺ) only met him twice; the first time was briefly before his prophetic mission and the second occasion was when the Prophet (ﷺ) went to meet Waraqah after receiving the first revelation from God. Waraqah died three years later. The revelation of the Qur'an, however, continued for 23 years.

Some of Muhammad's (ﷺ) pagan opponents accused him of learning the Qur'an from a Roman blacksmith, a Christian who was staying on the outskirts of Makkah. A revelation of the Qur'an was sufficient to refute this charge. Allah said:

❨And We surely know that they say, 'It is only a man that teaches him.' The tongue of the one they refer to is foreign, while this [*Qur'an*] is in a clear Arabic language.⟩ [16:103]

Muhammad's enemies kept a close watch on him, with the hope of uncovering a shred of evidence to support their claim that he was a liar. But they could not point to a single instance when the Prophet (ﷺ) might have had secret meetings with any particular Jews or Christians.

It is true that the Prophet (ﷺ) did have religious discussions with Jews and Christians, but they took place openly in Madinah, and the revelation of the Qur'an had been going on for more than 13 years before that. The allegation that these Jews and Christians were its source is groundless, especially since the role of Prophet Muhammad (ﷺ) was merely that of a teacher; he openly invited them to embrace Islam, pointing out how they had deviated from God's true teaching of monotheism. Numerous Jews and Christians embraced Islam themselves upon hearing Muhammad's (ﷺ) message.

In addition, it was known that Muhammad was unlettered. In His divine wisdom, Allah chose His final Messenger to be an unlettered man so no one would have the slightest justification to doubt him or accuse him of writing or copying the Qur'an.[8] Moreover, there was no Arabic version of the Bible in existence at the time of Prophet Muhammad (ﷺ). The earliest Arabic version of the Old Testament is that of R. Saadias Gaon of 900 C.E. - more than 250 years after the death of Muhammad (ﷺ).

We have mentioned that the Qur'an contains scientific miracles, and we presented a few facts stated within the book to evidence that it could not possibly have been known at that time by Muhammad or by any other person for that matter. More and more recent scientific discoveries are being found to coincide with what is stated in the Qur'an, and this is irrefutable evidence that its source was none but the all-knowing God - Allah, the Almighty.

It is true that there are some similarities between the Qur'an and the Bible, but this is not sufficient grounds to accuse Muhammad (ﷺ) of compiling or copying from the Bible. The similarities between the two do not indicate that later prophets plagiarized from previous ones, but merely point to a common source, who is the one true God, and to the continuation of the basic message of monotheism.

---

[8] The coming of the unlettered Prophet (ﷺ) was prophesized in the Bible: "*And the book is delivered to him that is not learned.*" [Isaiah 29:12]

8) How does the Qur'an differ from other scriptures?

It is an article of faith for every Muslim to believe in all the prophets and messengers of Allah and all unadulterated revelations of God. Some of these scriptures are still extant today but not in their pristine form as a result of human alteration. The Qur'an is the only divine scripture which has stood the test of time because Allah has taken upon Himself the responsibility of preserving it. He, the Exalted says:

《Indeed, it is We who have sent down the Reminder [i.e. the *Qur'an*], and indeed, We will be its guardian.》 [15:9]

Other revealed scriptures before the advent of Prophet Muhammad (ﷺ), such as the Old Testament and the Gospel, were recorded long after the demise of the prophets to whom they had been revealed. In contrast, the entire Qur'an was written down in its complete form during the lifetime of Muhammad (ﷺ) on pieces of palm bark, leather parchment and bone, and arranged in the order designated by the Prophet (ﷺ). In addition, tens of thousands of the Prophet's companions committed it to memory as it was being revealed. The Qur'an is still memorized and read in its original Arabic text, and it continues to be taught and learned by millions of people the world over. In fact, with every succeeding generation of Muslims, the number of those who commit the whole Qur'an to memory has incredibly increased. There is no other book, religious or otherwise, which has been given this unparalleled care in recorded history.

The Qur'an presents all the prophets of Allah as belonging to one single brotherhood; all had a similar prophetic mission and conveyed the same basic message, namely, the invitation to the worship of Allah alone. The source of their message was one: Allah, or Almighty God. Even if the other Scriptures agree with the Qur'an in the fundamental aspects of the religion, they address a specific people. Due to this, its rulings and regulations are particular to them. It is attributed to Jesus (عَلَيْهِ السَّلَام) in the Bible that he himself said:

"I was sent only to the lost sheep of the house (children) of Israel." [*Matthew* 15:24]

On the other hand, the Qur'an was revealed to humanity at large and not to any specific nation. Allah says:

❨**And We have not sent you** [O Muhammad (ﷺ)] **except to all of mankind, as a giver of glad tidings and a Warner, but most people know not.**❩ [34:28]

Jesus, the Messenger of Allah

9) **Is it correct that Muslims do not believe in Jesus or other Prophets?**

A Muslim cannot be a Muslim if he or she does not believe in Jesus (عليه السلام). Muslims believe in Jesus and in all of Allah's prophets. It is a basic element of their faith to believe in all of His prophets and messengers. Muslims respect and revere Jesus (عليه السلام) and await his second coming. According to the Qur'an, he was not crucified but was raised into Heaven. Muslims consider Jesus (عليه السلام) among the prominent messengers of Allah - but not God or the son of God. Jesus' mother, Mary is considered a virtuous and noble woman, and the Qur'an tells us that Jesus was born miraculously without a father:

﴿Indeed, the example of Jesus with Allah is like that of Adam. He created him from dust, and then He said to him, 'Be!' and he was.﴾ [3:59]

Many non-Muslims are surprised to find out that Islam considers, Jesus, the son of Mary, to be one of the greatest messengers of Allah. Muslims are taught to love Jesus, and a person cannot be a Muslim without believing in the virgin birth and in the miracles of Jesus Christ (عليه السلام). Muslims believe these things about Jesus not because of the Bible, but because the Qur'an says these things about him. However, Muslims always emphasize that the miracles of Jesus, and of all other prophets, were only possible by "Allah's permission" and His will.

Muslims reject the idea that Allah has a son. The Qur'an stresses emphatically that God does not have a "son". Islam teaches that titles such as "Lord" and "Savior" are for Allah alone.

It should be clarified that when Muslims criticize some of the teachings of Christianity, they are not attacking Jesus Christ (عليه السلام). Christian doctrines such as the "Trinity" and "Atonement" are criticized by Muslims simply because they did not originate from Jesus (عليه السلام). And when they evaluate the Bible they are not referring to "God's word", but to writings that are claimed to be God's word. Muslims believe that the book known today as "The Bible" only contains remnants of God's original messages, and that it has been tainted by human input and altered through numerous translations. Muslims believe the original Gospel was the words and teachings of Jesus, not those of the 'disciples', Paul or other church fathers who strongly influenced Christianity throughout history. Islam actually endorses Jesus (عليه السلام) when it insists on the pure monotheism that Jesus himself preached and followed.

10) **What does the Qur'an say about Jesus (ﷺ)?**

Jesus (ﷺ) was among the prominent messengers who were mentioned in detail in the Qur'an. In fact, there is a chapter in the Qur'an named *Maryam* (Mary) that speaks about Mary and her son Jesus (ﷺ). Jesus (ﷺ) is also mentioned in various other places throughout the Qur'an. Here are some of the Qur'anic quotations regarding Mary and Jesus:

❨**And relate in the Book** [the story of] **Mary, when she withdrew in seclusion from her family to a place facing east. She took in seclusion from them a screen. Then We sent to her Our angel, and he appeared before her as a man in all respects. She said, 'Indeed, I seek refuge in the Most Merciful [God] from you, if you should fear Him.' He said, 'I am only the messenger of your Lord, to** [announce to] **you the gift of a pure son."** She said: **"How can I have a son when no man has touched me, nor am I unchaste?' He said: 'Thus** [it will be]. **Your Lord says, 'It is easy for Me, and We will make him a sign to mankind and a mercy from Us. And it is a matter** [already] **decreed.'" So she conceived him, and she withdrew with him to a remote place. And the pains of childbirth drove her to the trunk of a palm tree. She cried, 'Would that I had died before this, and had been forgotten!' Then** [Jesus] **called her from beneath her, 'Grieve not, for your Lord has provided a** stream beneath you. And shake towards you the trunk of the palm tree: it will let fresh ripe dates fall upon you. So eat and drink and be contented. And if you see any man, say, "I have vowed abstention to the Most Merciful, so this day I will not speak to any human being.' At length she brought him (Jesus) to her people, carrying him. They said, 'O Mary, you have done a thing unprecedented. O sister [i.e., descendant] of Aaron, your father was not a man of evil nor was your mother unchaste'. So she pointed to him. They said, 'How can we talk to a child who is [yet] in the cradle?' [Jesus] said: 'I am indeed a servant of Allah; He has given me the Scripture and made me a prophet. And He has made me blessed wherever I am and enjoined on me prayer and *Zakah* (charity) as long as I live. And [made me] kind to my mother and not a wretched tyrant. And peace is on me the day I was born, the day I die, and the day I am raised alive.' That is Jesus the son of Mary, the word of truth about which they dispute. It is not befitting for Allah to take a son. Exalted is He! When He decrees a matter, He only says to it, 'Be', and it is. Indeed, Allah is my Lord and your Lord, so worship Him. That is the straight path.⟩ [19:16-36]

Islam, science and health matters

11) Is Islam opposed to knowledge and science?

Islam is not opposed to knowledge and science. Knowledge is of two types: religious, which has to do with the understanding of the religious duties one is required to carry out, and temporal, which has to do with all that is needed to know with a view to living a comfortable and beneficial life. A Muslim is required to acquire both types of knowledge. In fact, Islam advocated attaining knowledge and education at a time when the whole world was engulfed in utter ignorance. The first revelation the Prophet of Islam (ﷺ) received from Allah was:

❮Read in the name of your Lord who created - created man from a clinging clot. Read, and your Lord is the most Generous, who taught by the pen; taught man that which he knew not.❯ [96:1-5]

These verses represent the first spark ever to dispel the darkness of ignorance and barbarianism in which the world had long been immersed. And Allah reminded the Muslims of His immeasurable favour to humankind, saying:

❮It is He who raised among the unlettered people a Messenger from among themselves, reciting to them His verses, purifying them and teaching them the Book and wisdom, although they were before in manifest error.⟩ [62:2]

The early generations of Muslims became, in a matter of years, a learned and refined nation in religious as well as worldly matters, after having remained in the darkness of ignorance for centuries. Islam awakened in man the faculty of intellect and motivated him to serve Allah, the one true God.

Religious knowledge is essential, because, without it, one will not be able to perform his or her obligations in the prescribed manner. The Prophet (ﷺ) said,

"To whomever He intends benefit, Allah grants understanding of the religion."

Allah ordered the Prophet (ﷺ) to pray to Him for advancement in knowledge:

⟨**Say: 'My Lord, increase me in knowledge.**⟩

[20:114]

Beneficial worldly knowledge is also necessary, and Muslims are encouraged to acquire it in order to benefit themselves and their fellow men. When the early Muslims understood this fact, they surpassed other nations in development and productivity and carried the torch of knowledge for many centuries.

Islam made great advances in the fields of medicine, mathematics, physics, astronomy, geography, architecture, art, literature, and history, to mention but a few. Many important new procedures such as the use of algebra, Arabic numerals, and the concept of the zero –which was vital to the advancement of mathematics-, were transmitted to medieval Europe from Muslim countries. It was the Muslims who developed sophisticated instruments, including the astrolabe, the quadrant and good navigational maps which were to make possible the European voyages of discovery to the New World.

As **T.W. Wallbank** and **A. Schrier** put it:

"In medicine, mathematics, astronomy, chemistry and physics, Muslim achievements were particularly noteworthy. Well-equipped hospitals, usually associated with medical schools, were located in the principal cities. At a time when superstition still hampered the practice of medicine in western countries, Muslim physicians were diagnosing diseases, prescribing cures and performing advanced surgery... Probably the greatest of all physicians was the 19th century figure, Al-Razi, known in the West as Rhazes. He was the author of scores of scientific works, including a comprehensive medical encyclopaedia and a pioneering handbook on smallpox and measles. A 10th century physician,

Avicenna, (Ibn Sina) compiled a huge *Cannon of Medicine* which was considered the standard guide in European medical circles until the late 17th century... Important advances were made in algebra, analytical geometry and plane spherical trigonometry."[9]

The Qur'an itself is a book of guidance and it contains some amazing scientific facts. They are amazing because although they were revealed to Prophet Muhammad (ﷺ) over 14 centuries ago, they were not really understood by man until scientists "discovered" them in very recent times. Although not meant to be a book of scientific facts as such, the Qur'an mentions certain realities that would only be recognized and appreciated through technological advancements in later centuries - further undeniable evidence and proof that it was not the work of Muhammad (ﷺ) or of any person, but divine revelation from God.

[9] *Living World History*, Scott Forseman and Company, 1990, p.191-2

12) **The Qur'an says that only Allah knows what is in the womb. Does this not contradict medical science?**

To answer this we should look at the verses that relate to this matter. Allah says:

❨**Verily Allah [alone] has knowledge of the Hour and sends down the rain and knows what is in the wombs.**❩ [31:34]

And He says:

❨**Allah knows what every female carries, and what the wombs lose [prematurely] or exceed. And everything with Him is by due measure.**❩

[13:8]

If one reads the Arabic text of this verse, they will find that there is no Arabic word that corresponds to the English word 'sex' or 'gender'. The Qur'an mentions only the knowledge of "what" is in the womb. Many have misunderstood this to mean the sex of the child in the womb, which is incorrect.

Today, science has indeed advanced, and we can easily determine the sex of the child in the womb of a pregnant mother using ultrasound scanning.

Therefore, the above verse refers to every aspect of the fetus' present and future existence. What will be the child's nature? Will the child be a blessing or a curse to the parents? What will happen to him or her throughout life? Will he or she do good or evil? How long will he or she live? Will he or she end up in Paradise or in Hell? Allah alone knows all of this... no scientist in the world, no matter how advanced the technology, will ever be able to determine these things about a child in the mother's womb.

13) **The Qur'an mentions that human beings are created from dust and it also mentions that they are created from sperm. Isn't this contradictory?**

Allah has said:

❨And We made from water every living thing.❩

[21:30]

And He said:

❨Indeed, We created you from dust.❩ [22:5]

And He said:

❨Indeed We have created them from sticky clay.❩ [37:11]

In the preceding verses, Allah has mentioned various stages of human creation. The creation of man according to the Qur'an was first from water and dust, which when combined became clay. This refers to the creation of humanity's first ancestor, Adam (ﷺ). Then Allah decreed that his descendants would reproduce after that according to the same natural law that is applied to many other living beings.

Sometimes the Qur'an refers to semen as "water", meaning fluid. So when Allah says in the Qur'an that He created every living thing from water, it can indicate that everything in creation; humans, animals and plants have all been created from water and depend upon water for their continued existence. But a similar verse: ❨And Allah has created every creature from water.❩[10] can also mean that human beings and animals are created from their fathers' semen or sperm. This is confirmed by other verses, such as: ❨Did We not create you from a liquid disdained?❩[11]

As for scientific evidence, research has confirmed that the body of man, like that of other living beings, is made up predominantly of water, and that the elements of the human body are exactly the same as those found in the earth's soil in greater or smaller quantities.

---

[10] 24:45
[11] 77:20.

14) Why is the consumption of alcohol prohibited in Islam?

In Islam all things that are harmful or whose harm exceeds their benefit are unlawful. Therefore, alcohol would be deemed unlawful in Islam even if it were not clearly prohibited in the Qur'an and prophetic traditions. For anything that causes harm is considered unlawful.

Alcohol has been the scourge of human society since time immemorial. It continues to cost countless human lives, and causes misery to millions throughout the world. Statistics showing soaring crime rates, increasing instances of mental illnesses and millions of broken homes throughout the world bear witness to the destructive power of alcohol.

Alcohol incapacitates the inhibitory center in the human brain. That is the reason that an inebriated person is often found to be indulging in behavior that is completely uncharacteristic. A drunkard finds it difficult to talk or walk properly. He may even urinate in his clothes. If a person should become intoxicated and commits something shameful just once, it may possibly remain with him the rest of his life.

There are a number of medical reasons for the prohibition of the consumption of alcohol. Millions of people die every year as a result of it. A few of the alcohol related illnesses are:

* Cirrhosis of liver

* Various forms of cancer

* Oesophagitis, gastritis and pancreatitis

*Cardiomyopathy, hypertension, angina and heart attacks

* Strokes, apoplexy, fits and different types of paralysis

* Peripheral neuropathy, cortical atrophy, cerebelar atrophy

* Numerous endocrine disorders

* Anemia, jaundice and platelet abnormalities

* Recurrent chest infections, pneumonia, emphysema and pulmonary tuberculosis

* During pregnancy, alcohol consumption has a severe detrimental effect on the fetus

Many claim that they only have one or two drinks and exercise self-control and so they never get intoxicated. But investigations reveal that every alcoholic started as a social drinker. Not a single alcoholic or drunkard initially starts drinking with the intention of becoming an alcoholic. It just happens along the way.

Allah, in His infinite wisdom, made injunctions aimed at preserving the individual and society. Hence the consumption of alcohol is prohibited in

Islam. It is worth mentioning that when Muslims refrain from doing things that Allah has forbidden, they do not do so because of detrimental effects but because Allah has prohibited them. Their aim in this world is to obey Allah's commands, and by doing so they also benefit themselves.

Women in Islam

15) Does Islam oppress women?

In answering this question, we must differentiate between the teachings of Islam and the practice of some Muslims. Although some Muslim cultures oppress women, it often reflects local customs that are inconsistent, if not contrary to Islamic teachings. Islam expects its adherents to uphold the rights of women, to protect their social status and prevent their degradation in every way. Islam further holds that women are equal to men in their origin, their humanity, their honor and their accountability before God.

Today, Western societies have actually demoted women to sex objects. The United States of America is one of the leading advocates of the so-called "women's liberation" movement. Ironically, it also has one of the highest rates of sexual assault and rape in the world. According to an FBI report, in the year 1990, an average of 1756 rapes were committed in the US every single day.

The idea that Islam treats women as second class citizens worth half a man is nothing but a myth. Islam elevated the status of women over 1,400 years ago by declaring them the sisters of men, giving them the right to education to the highest level, the right to choose a husband, the right to end an unhappy marriage, the right to inheritance, in general, the rights of a full citizen of the state. Not only material and physical rights, but those of kindness and consideration are equally specified and significant in Islamic law.

Men and women are two equally important component parts of humanity, and the rights and responsibilities of both sexes are equitable and balanced in their totality. Roles of men and women are complementary and collaborative. Although their obligations might differ in certain areas of life in accordance with their basic physical and psychological differences, each is equally accountable for their particular responsibilities. Ignoring these differences is surely unrealistic, but there is no reason to assume from them that one sex is either superior or inferior to the other in any way.

Under Islamic law, when a Muslim woman gets married she does not surrender her maiden name, but keeps her distinct identity.

In a Muslim marriage, the groom gives a dowry to the bride herself, and not to her father. This becomes her own personal property to keep, invest or spend, and is not subject to the dictates of any of her male relatives. The Qur'an places on men the responsibility of protecting and maintaining all of their female relatives. It means, as well, that a man must provide for his wife and family even if she has money of her own. She is not obligated to spend any of her money towards the maintenance of her family. This relieves a woman of the need to earn a living, but she can work if she chooses to do so or if her circumstances warrant it.

The family, like any other organization, needs order and leadership. The Qur'an states that the husband has a "degree" of authority over his wife, which means guardianship. It is important to note, however, that guardianship is in no way a license to be a tyrant within the household. Rather, it is a burden of responsibility for the husband to care completely for his wife and children.

16) Why do Muslim women wear the veil?

The matter of women's dress might seem trivial to some, especially in today's Western societies; however, Islam assigns to it moral, social and legal dimensions. Islam has defined the roles of men and women by allocating certain duties to each and granting certain rights to each. This is in order to maintain a proper balance in society. When men and women observe the proper Islamic dress, they not only protect their own honor and reputation, but they contribute greatly towards peace and order in society.

In general, there are certain guidelines concerning Muslim women's dress. Their garments should not be tight or translucent as to reveal the shape of what is covered. They must cover their entire bodies except the hands and face. This mode of dress is called "Jilbaab" which refers to a woman's outer garment, with which she is entirely covered. Muslim women do not dress modestly in obedience to their fathers, brothers or husbands, but only in obedience to God's commandments.

Both men and women are expected to be chaste and modest and avoid any type of dress and conduct that may invite temptation. Both are instructed to look only at what is lawful for them to see and to guard their chastity. Allah directs men first and then women in the Qur'an:

❨Tell the believing men to lower their gaze and guard their chastity. That is purer for them. Indeed, Allah is acquainted with what they do. And tell the believing women to lower their gaze and guard their chastity and not display their beauty except what [must ordinarily] appear thereof; and to wrap part of their head covers over their chests and not display their beauty except to their husbands, their fathers, their husbands' fathers, their sons, their husbands' sons, their brothers or their brothers' sons, or their sisters' sons.❩ [24:30-1]

The additional requirement for women to conceal their adornment and natural beauty is due to their greater need for privacy and protection. Except in the company of close relatives, a woman is required to cover her entire body with loose fitting garments with the exception of her face and hands.

The Qur'an states why Allah has prescribed particular dress regulations for women:

◁O Prophet, tell your wives and daughters and the women of the believers to draw over themselves their outer garments [when in public]. That is more suitable so they will be known (to be pious believing free women) and not be abused...▷ [33:59]

17) Why does Islam permit polygamy?

Polygamy is a form of marriage wherein a person has more than one spouse. Polygamy can be of two types. The first type is called polygyny, where a man marries more than one woman, and the other is polyandry, where a woman marries more than one man. In Islam, a limited form of polygyny is permitted, whereas polyandry is completely prohibited.

In contrast to Islam, one will not find a limit for the number of wives in the Jewish Talmud or the Christian Bible. According to these scriptures, there is no limit to how many women a man may marry. Therefore, polygyny is not something exclusive to Islam but was practiced by early Christians and Jews as well. According to the Talmud, Abraham had three wives, while King Solomon had hundreds of wives. The practice of polygyny continued in Judaism until Rabbi Gershom ben Yehudah (955-1030 CE) issued an edict against it. The Jewish Sephardic communities continued the practice until as late as 1950, when an Act of the Chief Rabbinate of Israel extended the ban on marrying more than one wife, thus prohibiting the practice for all Jews. In the early teachings of Christianity, men were permitted to take as many wives as they wished, since the Bible placed no limit on the number of wives a man could marry. It was only in recent centuries that the Church limited the number of wives to one.

At a time when men were permitted an unlimited number of wives, Islam limited the number to a maximum of four. Before the Qur'an was revealed, there was no upper limit for polygyny and many men had scores of wives. It gives a man permission to marry two, three or four women, on the condition that he deals with all of them equitably, benevolently and justly, as indicated by Allah's statement:

❨But if you fear that you will not be just, then marry only one.❩ [4:3]

It is not incumbent upon Muslims to practice polygyny. In Islam, taking an additional wife is neither encouraged nor prohibited. Furthermore, a Muslim who has two, three or four wives may not be a better Muslim as compared to a Muslim who has only one wife.

John Esposito, a professor of religion and international affairs and Islamic studies at Georgetown University, writes: **"Although it is found in many religious and cultural traditions, polygamy is most often identified with Islam in the minds of Westerners. In fact, the Qur'an and Islamic Law sought to control and regulate the number of spouses rather than give free license."** He continues: **"The Qur'an allows a man to marry up to four wives, provided he can support and treat them all equally. Muslims regard this Qur'anic command as strengthening the status of women and the family, for it sought to ensure the welfare of single women and widows in a society whose male population was diminished by warfare, and to curb unrestricted polygamy."**[12]

There are certain circumstances which warrant the taking of another wife. For example, if there is a surplus of unmarried women in society, especially during times of war when widows are in need of

---

[12] John Esposito, *Islam: The Straight Path*, Oxford University, 1988, p. 97

shelter and care. Infant mortality rates among males are higher when compared to that of females. During wars, there are usually more men killed than women. Statistically, more men die due to accidents and diseases than women. The average life span of females is also generally longer than that of males. As a result at any given time in practically any given place, there is a shortage of men in comparison to women. Therefore, even if every single man got married to one woman, there would be millions of women who would still not be able to find a husband.

In Western society, it is not uncommon for a man to have girlfriends, or if he is married, to have extramarital affairs. Seldom is this practice scorned, despite the harms that stem from it. At the same time, polygyny is banned in western society although it produces none of these adverse effects; rather it preserves the honor and chastity of women. Within a second, third or fourth marriage the woman is a wife, not a mistress; she has a husband who is obligated by Islamic law to provide for her and her children, not a "boyfriend" who may one day cast her aside or deny knowing her if she becomes pregnant.

There is no doubt that a second wife who is lawfully married and treated with honor is better off than a mistress without any legal rights or social respect. Islam strictly prohibits and penalizes prostitution, fornication, and adultery and permits polygyny under strict conditions.

18) If a man is permitted to have more than one wife, then why can't a woman have more than one husband?

Islam teaches that Allah has created men and women as equals, but not as identical beings. They are different, physically, biologically and physiologically and each have different capabilities. Their roles and responsibilities are therefore different but they complement one another.

Some may object to a man having the right to more than one wife by insisting that, in fairness, women should also be able to practice polyandry. However, the following few points could be part of the reason behind its prohibition by God:

* One of the benefits of polygyny is that it solves the problem of women outnumbering men.

* In general, men are polygamous by nature while women are not.

* Islam assigns great importance to the recognition of parents, both the mother and father. When a man has more than one wife, the parents of children born in such marriages can easily be identified. But in the case of a woman marrying more than one husband, only the mother of children born within the marriage

would be known without resorting to laboratory tests. Psychologists tell us that children who do not know their parents, the father in particular, undergo severe mental disturbances and trauma, and often have unhappy childhoods.

19) Why does Islam impose such harsh punishments for sex outside marriage?

Punishment in Islam has a social purpose, which is to dissuade others from committing the same crime. The nature of the punishment depends on the seriousness of the crime in question. Nowadays, some are opposed to the Islamic punishment for fornication and adultery because they see it as disproportionate or too harsh a punishment. The basic problem here is the different standards by which the severity of the crime is measured.

Islam views adultery as a very serious crime, because it undermines the very foundation of the family system upon which the whole superstructure of the society is built. Illicit relationships destabilize the family and bring about the breakdown of the system. Family breakdown imperils the physical and mental health of future generations, which in turn leads to a vicious circle of decadence, dissipation, and dissolution. Therefore, it is imperative that all measures must be taken to protect the family. That is why Islam emphasizes protection of the family by imposing severe punishments for activities that threaten the family foundation. These punishments are the same for men and women alike.

There is no overstating of the fact that Islamic punishments are only a part of a vastly larger integrated whole. There are essential conditions for the application of prescribed punishments in Islam:

* First, Muslims are strongly encouraged to marry whenever possible, providing a lawful means of gratification. Prophet Muhammad (ﷺ) said:

'O youths, whoever of you can afford marriage [financially and physically] **let him get married; for indeed it lowers the gaze, and keeps one chaste; whoever cannot get married, he should fast, for it safeguards him.'**

A man may legally take as many as four wives as long as he treats each of them equitably and justly. In cases of confirmed incompatibility or dissatisfaction, a wife has the right to request the dissolution of the marriage.

* Second, Muslims, whether married or unmarried, must adhere to proper dress and behavior guidelines at all times. Privacy is to be respected and compromising situations strictly avoided as a matter of obedience to Allah.

* Third, only a legitimate Islamic government has the right to implement these punishments. Such an Islamic government must establish justice as its core value in all affairs so that the social and cultural environment of the country is congenial for the moral life of its citizens. It is only after the above two conditions have been fulfilled that a government is entitled to implement Islamic punishments on its land, and only then does the court gain the authority to judge a case according to its provisions.

* And finally, any case that comes before the court for judgment must be investigated thoroughly and proper evidence brought before the court to satisfy all the requirements of Islamic law. Conviction is subject to strict conditions, which are most difficult to fulfill. This means that, in reality, the punishments are seldom carried out without the connivance of the criminal, and serve primarily as deterrents.

20) **Under Islamic law, why is a woman's share of inherited wealth half that of a man's?**

Islam abolished the former practice whereby inheritance went only to the oldest male heir. According to the Qur'an, a woman automatically inherits from her father, her husband, her son and her childless brother. The Qur'an contains specific guidance regarding the division of the inherited wealth among the rightful beneficiaries. The three verses that broadly describe the share of close relatives are found in *Surah an-Nisaa'*, verses 11, 12 and 176. In these verses, Allah establishes the right of children, parents and spouses to inherit a specific share without leaving the matter to human judgment and emotions. In the absence of certain close relatives a share is apportioned to more distant ones. The system of inheritance is a perfectly balanced product of the Creator's knowledge of human need and takes into account His imposition of greater responsibility upon particular members of the family in varying situations.

In most cases, the female inherits a share that is half that of the male. However, this is not always so. There are certain instances when they inherit equal shares, and in some cases, a female can inherit a share that is more than that of the male. But even when the male is given a larger share there is a perfectly logical reason behind it. In Islam a woman has no financial obligations towards her family, even if she is wealthy or has her own source of income; the economic responsibility always lies upon the man. As long as a woman remains unmarried, it is the legal obligation of her father, brother or other guardian to provide her food, clothing, medication, housing and other financial needs. After she is married, it is the duty of her husband or adult son. Islam holds the man financially responsible for fulfilling all the needs of his family.

So the difference in shares does not mean that one sex is preferred over the other. It represents a just balance between the roles and responsibilities of family members according to their natural, physical and emotional makeup. In general, the woman is in charge of running the household and taking care of the needs of those within it, so she is alleviated from financial obligations. Despite this, she receives a share of inheritance which becomes her own property to save or use as she pleases. No other person has claim to any portion of her share. In contrast, the man's share becomes a part of his property from which he is obligated to maintain his children and all female members of the household, so it is constantly being consumed.

Suppose someone died leaving a son and a daughter. The son's share of inheritance will be depleted when he gives a dowry to his wife and supports his family, including his sister until she marries. Any additional income will have to be earned through his work. However, his sister's share remains untouched, or might even increase if she invests it. When she marries, she will receive a dowry from her husband and will be maintained by him, having no financial responsibilities whatsoever. Thus, a man might conclude that Islam has favored women over men!

In addition, the Muslim may make a bequest at his own discretion, in which he can will up to one third of his property to anyone who would not inherit otherwise. The bequest can be a means of assistance to other relatives and people in need, both men and women. One may also allocate this portion or part of it toward charities and good works of his choice.

Islam and Terrorism

21) What is "*Jihad*"?

While Islam is generally misunderstood in the West, perhaps no other Islamic term evokes such strong reactions as "jihad". The Arabic word *"Jihad"*, which is most always mistranslated as "holy war", simply means "to struggle" or "to exert one's utmost effort". It is incorrect to imagine that jihad is synonymous only with fighting or war, for this is but one particular aspect of the term.[13] Jihad is a struggle to do good and to remove injustice, oppression and evil from oneself and from society. This struggle is spiritual, social, economic and political.

Indeed, the concept of jihad is one of life, and it is vast, not limited only to armed conflict. For example, one finds in the Qur'an mention of "jihad by means of the Qur'an",[14] meaning invitation to the truth, evidence, clarification and presenting the best argument. There is also "jihad of the soul", which means striving to purify the soul, to increase its faith and incline it toward good while keeping it from evil and from unlawful desires and temptations. Then there is "jihad through wealth", which means spending it in various beneficial ways, including

---

[13] The word for war in the Qur'an is *"harb"* or *"qitaal"*.
[14] Refer to 25:52

charities and welfare projects. And there is "jihad through the self", which comprises all good works done by a believer, such as propagation, teaching and finally, lawful armed struggle against aggression and oppression.

In the name of jihad, Islam calls for the protection of societies from oppression, foreign domination and dictatorships that usurp rights and freedom, that abolish just and moral rule, that prevent people from hearing the truth or following it, and that practice religious persecution. In the name of jihad, it endeavors to teach belief in Allah, the One supreme God, and worship of Him and to spread good values, virtue and morality through wise and proper methods. Allah has commanded:

❨Invite to the way of your Lord with wisdom and good instruction, and argue with them in a way that is best.❩ [16:125]

In the name of jihad, Islam calls for social reform and the elimination of ignorance, superstition, poverty, disease and racial discrimination. Among its main goals is the protection of rights for weaker members of society against the impositions of the powerful and influential.

Islam prohibits injustice, even toward those who oppose the religion. Allah, the Exalted, says in the Qur'an:

❨And do not let the hatred of a people prevent you from being just. Be just; that is nearer to righteousness.❩ [5:8]

And Allah told the believers regarding those who prevented their entry to the Sacred Mosque in Makkah:

❨And do not let the hatred of a people for having obstructed you from the Sacred Mosque lead you to transgress.❩ [5:2]

Enmity toward any people or nation should not provoke Muslims to commit aggression against them, oppress them or disregard their rights.

One of the highest levels of jihad is to stand up to a tyrant and speak a word of truth. Restraining the self from wrongdoing is also a great form of jihad. Another form of jihad is to take up arms in defense of Islam or a Muslim country when Islam is attacked, but this has to be declared by the religious leadership or by a Muslim head of state.

Although Jihad is a wider concept than war, it is also clear that Islam acknowledges war when it becomes the last option for the treatment of such problems as oppression and aggression and for the defense of certain freedoms and rights. When Islam acknowledges military engagement, it is as an integral part of a complete system of values inherent in the religion, behind which any equitable person can perceive the reason and logic.

War is permissible in Islam only when all peaceful means such as dialogue, negotiations and treaties fail. War is a last resort and should be avoided as much as possible. The purpose of Jihad is not to convert people by force, or to colonize people or to acquire land or wealth or for self-glory. Its purpose is basically the defense of life, property, land, honor and freedom for oneself as well as defense of others from injustice and oppression.

22) Is Islam a militant religion?

In Islam, the use of force is allowed only in special situations, particularly when the Muslim community is threatened by hostile forces. This is indeed natural and logical for any nation. Then again, the use of force in a campaign of jihad is determined by the leader of the Muslim community in a very ordered and ethical way.

Islam considers all life forms as sacred, but particularly emphasizes the sanctity of human life. Allah says in the Qur'an:

❨And do not kill the soul which Allah has forbidden [to be killed] except by [legal] right.❩

[6:151]

Allah says:

❨Whoever kills a soul unless for a soul[15] or for corruption [done] in the land[16] – it is as if he had slain all mankind. And whoever saves one – it is as if he had saved mankind entirely.❩ [5:32]

Such is the value of a single human life, that Allah equates the taking of even one human life unjustly with killing all of humanity.

It is important to understand that in Islam, war is only permitted in specific and dire circumstances. It is despised and only permitted as a last resort when all other attempts at peace have been made. It keeps warfare at a level of mercy and respect for the enemy such as none other has been able to reach. The Prophet (ﷺ), sometimes had to fight for the mere survival of his mission, but once security was ensured, he immediately reverted to peace and diplomacy.

---

[15]i.e., in legal retribution for murder.
[16]i.e., that requiring the death penalty.

Even in a state of war, Islam enjoins that armies deal with the enemy justly in the battlefield. Islam has drawn a clear line of distinction between the combatants and the non-combatants of an enemy country. The Prophet (ﷺ) told his armies,

"Do not kill any old person, any child or any woman."[17]

And He said:

"Do not kill the monks in monasteries."[18]

Upon seeing the corpse of a woman on a battlefield, Prophet Muhammad (ﷺ) angrily asked his companions why she had been killed, and he strongly condemned the atrocious act. For those enemies active in combat and those taken as prisoners of war, the list of rights is lengthy. There should be no torture; no killing of the wounded or defenseless, no mutilation of enemy bodies and return of corpses to the enemy must be honored. In light of the aforementioned, it becomes crystal clear that Islam does not permit aggression, violence, injustice, or oppression. At the same time, it calls for morality, justice, tolerance, and peace.

---

[17] Narrated by Abu Dawud.
[18] Narrated by Ahmad.

Far from being a militant dogma, Islam is a way of life that transcends race and ethnicity. The Qur'an repeatedly reminds us of our common origin:

〈O mankind, indeed We created you from male and a female, and made you peoples and tribes that you may know one another. Verily the most noble of you in the sight of Allah is the most righteous of you.〉 [49:13]

It is the universality of its teachings that makes Islam the fastest growing religion in the world. In a world full of conflicts and deep schisms between human beings, a world that is currently plagued with terrorism, perpetrated by individuals and by states, Islam is a beacon of light that offers hope for the future.

23) Are Muslims terrorists?

It is very unfortunate that nowadays, Islam has become synonymous with "terrorism". Far from promoting terrorism, Islam is a religion of peace whose fundamentals teach its followers to maintain and promote peace and justice throughout the world. Islam does not condone "terrorism" as defined and understood nowadays: plane hijackings, hostage taking and the torturing and killing of innocents in order to achieve political or even religious goals. This is not how Islam teaches Muslims to solve their problems, achieve their goals, or to spread their religion.

The question that should be posed instead is: Do the teachings of Islam encourage terrorism? Certainly not - Islam totally prohibits all terrorist acts. It should be remembered that all religions have misguided followers. To be evenhanded and just, one must consider the teachings of the religion, as they are the yardstick by which the actions of its adherents can be assessed as being right or wrong.

It is completely unfair to judge Islam by the wrongdoings of some misguided or ignorant Muslims, or by the deteriorating condition of Muslims and the blatant corruption that pervades the Muslim world. In fact, what Islam preaches is one thing and what so many Muslims nowadays practice is something completely different. The only way we can do justice to Islam is to find out about its noble teachings, which are clearly set out in the Qur'an and prophetic traditions. Former pop singer Cat Stevens, now known as Yousef Islam, observed: **"It is wrong to judge Islam in the light of the behavior of some deviant Muslims who are always shown on the media. It is like judging a car to be bad if the driver is drunk and he crashes it into a wall."**

Islam is a religion of peace, which is acquired by submitting one's will to the will of the supreme Creator, God. Islam promotes peace but at the same time, it exhorts its followers to fight oppression. The fight against oppression may, at times, require the use of force, and sometimes force has to be used to maintain peace.

Certainly, Islamic law allows war under particular circumstances. Any religion or civilization that does not, would never survive. But Islam never condones attacks against innocent people, women or children. Islam also clearly forbids *"taking the law into one's own hands"*, which means that individual Muslims cannot go around deciding who they want to kill or punish. Trial and punishment must only be carried out by a lawful authority and a qualified judge.

24) How can Islam be called a "religion of peace" when it was "spread by the sword"?

It is another common misconception among some non-Muslims that Islam would not have the millions of adherents it has all over the world, had it not been spread by the use of force.

The following proofs will make it clear, that far from being forcefully "spread by the sword", it was the inherent force of truth, reason and logic that was responsible for the rapid spread of Islam.

* Islam has always given respect and freedom of religion to all faiths. Freedom of religion is ordained in the Qur'an itself:

{There shall be no compulsion in [acceptance of] the religion. The right course has become clear from the wrong.} [2:256]

The noted historian De Lacy O'Leary wrote:[19] "History makes it clear however, that the legend of fanatical Muslims sweeping through the world and forcing Islam at the point of the sword upon conquered races is one of the most fantastically absurd myths that historians have ever repeated."

Another famous historian, Thomas Carlyle, in his book *Heroes and Hero worship*, refers to this misconception about the spread of Islam: "The sword indeed, but where will you get your sword? Every new opinion, at its starting is precisely in a minority of one; in one man's head alone. There it dwells as yet. One man alone of the whole world believes it, there is one man against all men. That he takes a sword and tries to propagate with that will do little for him. You must get your sword! On the whole, a thing will propagate itself as it can."

---

[19] In his book *Islam at the Crossroads*, p.8.

If Islam was indeed spread by the sword, it was the sword of intellect and convincing arguments that was used. It is only this type of sword that conquers the hearts and minds of people. The Qur'an says in this connection:

《Invite to the way of your Lord with wisdom and good instruction, and argue with them in a way that is best.》 [16:125]

The facts speak for themselves:

* Indonesia is the country that has the largest number of Muslims in the world, and the majority of people in Malaysia are Muslims. But, no Muslim army ever entered Indonesia or Malaysia. It is an established historical fact that Indonesia entered Islam not due to war, but because of its moral message. Despite the disappearance of Islamic government from many regions once ruled by it, their original inhabitants have remained Muslims. Moreover, they carried the message of truth, inviting others to it as well, and in so doing endured harm, affliction and oppression. The same can be said for those in the regions of Syria and Jordan, Egypt, Iraq, North Africa, Asia, the Balkans and in Spain. This shows that the effect of Islam on the population was one of moral conviction, in contrast to occupation by western colonialists, finally compelled to leave lands

whose peoples held only memories of affliction, sorrow, subjugation and oppression.

* Muslims ruled Spain (Andalusia) for about 800 years. During this period, the Christians and Jews enjoyed freedom to practice their respective religions, and this is a documented historical fact.

* Christian and Jewish minorities have survived in the Muslim lands of the Middle East for centuries. Countries such as Egypt, Morocco, Palestine, Lebanon, Syria, and Jordan all have significant Christian and Jewish populations.

* Muslims ruled India for about a thousand years, and therefore had the power to force each and every non-Muslim resident of India to convert to Islam, but they did not, and thus more than 80% of the Indian population remains non-Muslim.

* Similarly, Islam spread rapidly on the East Coast of Africa. And likewise no Muslim army was ever dispatched to the East Coast of Africa.

* An article in *Reader's Digest* 'Almanac', yearbook 1986, gives the statistics of the increase of the percentage of the major religions of the world in half a century from 1934 to 1984. This article also

appeared in The *Plain Truth* magazine. At the top was Islam, which increased by 235%, while Christianity had increased by 47%. During this fifty-year period, there was no "Islamic conquest" yet Islam spread at such an extraordinary rate.

* Today, the fastest growing religion in North America, Europe, and Africa is Islam. The Muslims in most of these lands constitute a minority. The only sword they have in their possession is the sword of truth. It is this sword that is converting thousands to Islam.

* Islamic law protects the privileged status of minorities, and that is why non-Muslim places of worship have flourished all over the Islamic world. Islamic law also allows non-Muslim minorities to set up their own courts, which implement family laws drawn up by the minorities themselves. The life and property of all citizens in an Islamic state are considered sacred whether they are Muslims or not.

It is clear, therefore, that Islam was not spread by the sword. The often-alleged "sword of Islam" did not convert all the non-Muslim minorities in Muslim countries. In India, where Muslims ruled for about a thousand years, they are still a minority. In the U.S.A. and Canada Islam is the fastest growing religion and has over seven million followers.

In his book *The World's Religions*, Huston Smith discusses how the Prophet Muhammad (ﷺ) granted freedom of religion to the Jews and Christians under Muslim rule:

The Prophet had a document drawn up in which he stipulated that Jews and Christians "shall be protected from all insults and harm; they shall have an equal right with our own people to our assistance and good offices," and further, "they shall practice their religion as freely as the Muslims."[20]

Smith points out that Muslims regard that document as the first charter of freedom of conscience in human history and the authoritative model for those of every subsequent Muslim state.

25) **The Qur'an says that Muslims should kill the non-believers wherever they find them. Does this mean that Islam promotes violence, bloodshed and brutality?**

There are a few verses from the Qur'an that are quite often misquoted or quoted out of context to perpetuate the myth that Islam promotes violence and exhorts its followers to kill those outside the fold

---

[20] Quoted in *The World's Religions* by Huston Smith, Harper Collins, 1991, p. 256

of Islam. The words ⟨**Kill the polytheists wherever you find them**⟩ are often quoted to portray that Islam promotes violence, bloodshed and brutality.

In order to understand the context, it is necessary to read from the beginning of the chapter. It discloses that there was a peace treaty between the Muslims and the pagans of Makkah. The pagans violated this treaty, so a period of four months was given them to make amends; otherwise war would be declared against them. The complete verse actually says:

⟨**But when the sacred months have passed, then kill the polytheists wherever you find them and seize them and besiege them, and lie in wait for them at every place of ambush. But if they should repent, establish prayer and *give Zakah*, then open the way for them. Indeed, Allah is Forgiving and Merciful.**⟩ [9:5]

This verse is a command to the Muslims who had entered into an agreement with the pagans, who soon violated the agreement, to fight and kill those who betrayed them wherever they found them. It would seem that any open-minded person would consider the historical context of this verse and agree that it cannot be used as "evidence" that Islam promotes violence, brutality and bloodshed, or that it exhorts its followers to kill anyone outside the fold of Islam.

The very next verse gives the answer to the allegation that Islam promotes violence, brutality and bloodshed.[21] It says:

❨If any one of the pagans asks you for asylum, then grant it to him so that he may hear the words of Allah [i.e., the Qur'an]. Then escort him to where he is safe. That is because they are a people who do not know.❩ [9:6]

The Qur'an not only stipulates that a pagan seeking asylum during the battle should be granted refuge, but also that he be escorted to safety. In the present age, what military commander would direct his soldiers not just to spare an enemy during battle, but to escort him to a place of safety? Yet, that is exactly what Almighty Allah instructs in the Qur'an.

---

[21] Arun Shourie, one of the most persistent critics of Islam in India, quotes the same verse (9:5) in his book, *The World of Fatwas*, p. 572. But after quoting it, he skips the next verse and jumps to the one after it. This is a clear indication that some of the opponents of Islam are biased and prejudiced in their criticism.

Universality of the Message of Islam

26)   Is it true that Islam is a religion only for Arabs?

This idea can be easily be disproved, as only about 15 to 20 percent of Muslims in the world are Arabs. There are more Indian Muslims than Arab Muslims, and more Indonesian Muslims than Indian Muslims. This assumption is possibly based on the fact that most of the first generation of Muslims were Arabs, that the Qur'an is in Arabic and that the Prophet Muhammad (ﷺ) was an Arab.

However, history testifies that the Prophet (ﷺ), his followers and the early Muslims made every effort to spread the message of Islam to all nations, races and peoples. From the very beginning of the mission of Prophet Muhammad (ﷺ) his followers came from a wide spectrum of countries and races. Among them was Bilal, the African slave; Suhaib, the Byzantine Roman; Abdullah bin Salam, the Jewish Rabbi; and Salman, the Persian.

Furthermore, it should be clarified that not all Muslims are Arabs and not all Arabs are Muslims. An Arab might be a Muslim, Christian, Jew, atheist or follower of any other religion or ideology. Additionally, some countries - such as Turkey and Iran (Persia) - that uninformed people consider to be "Arab" are not Arab at all. The people who live in those countries speak languages other than Arabic and are of a different ethnic heritage.

Since religious truth is eternal and unchanging, and humanity is considered one universal brotherhood, Islam teaches that God's revelations to humanity have always been consistent, clear and universal. The truth of Islam is meant for all people regardless of race, nationality, cultural or linguistic background. A brief look at the Muslim World, from Nigeria to Bosnia and from Malaysia to Afghanistan is sufficient proof that Islam offers a universal appeal; a message for all of mankind - not to mention the fact that significant numbers of Europeans and Americans of all races and ethnic backgrounds are finding and coming into Islam. The Qur'an clearly says,

《And We have not sent you (O Muhammad) except as a giver of glad tidings and a warner to all mankind, but most men know not.》 [34:28]

27) All religions basically teach their followers to do good deeds, so why should a person follow Islam?

In the Qur'an, Allah says,

《This day, I have perfected for you your religion, completed My favor upon you, and have chosen for you Islam as your religion.》 [5:3]

He also says,

《Truly, the religion with Allah is Islam.》 [3:19]

And He says,

《And whosoever seeks a religion other than Islam never will it be accepted from him, and in the Hereafter he will be among the losers.》 [3:85]

Islam is Allah's final message, and it offers a complete legal code for humankind. It eliminates and corrects the human errors that found their way into previous religions in the realm of both belief and practice. Just as any new revised law supersedes and nullifies what came before it, Islam naturally abrogates all earlier religions.

Without doubt, one will find in every religion, especially those of divine origins, such as Judaism, Christianity and Islam, noble teachings, good moral values, encouragement toward good deeds and warnings against evil. However, what distinguishes Islam from other faiths is that Islam goes beyond simply urging people to be upright and honest. Islam diagnoses illnesses and prescribes the treatment. It gives practical solutions to man's problems and provides the means of achieving righteousness and eliminating evil from individual and collective lives. Islam is guidance for mankind from the Creator who knows what is best and most suitable for His creation. That is why Islam is called the natural religion of man.

A Final Word

We would now like our readers to ask themselves what they think are the reasons for all the propaganda and misinformation currently being perpetuated about Islam. If Islam was just another false religion that made no sense, would so many feel a need to invent so many falsehoods about it? The reason is merely that the ultimate truth of Islam stands on unshakeable ground, and that its basic fundamental belief in the oneness of Allah is above reproach. Thomas Carlyle said:

A false man found a religion? Why, a false man cannot build a brick house! If he does not know and follow truly the properties of mortar, burnt clay and what else he works in, it is no house that he makes, but a rubbish-heap. It will not stand for twelve centuries, to lodge a hundred and eighty millions; it will fall straightway. A man must conform himself to Nature's laws, be verily in communion with Nature and the truth of things, or Nature will answer him, No, not at all! Speciosities are specious - ah me! - a Cagliostro, many Cagliostros, prominent world-leaders, do prosper by their quackery, for a day. It is like a forged bank-note; they get it passed out of their worthless hands: others, not they, have to

smart for it. Nature bursts up in fire-flames; French Revolutions and such like, proclaiming with terrible veracity that forged notes are forged. But of a Great Man especially, of him, I will venture to assert that it is incredible he should have been other than true. It seems to me the primary foundation of him, and of all that can lie in him, is this.[22]

Finally, we must never rely on second hand information to understand the religion of Islam. Rather, it needs to be studied from its authentic sources and by speaking to sincere, practicing Muslims. By rereading the introductory section of this book, one will surely find a different picture than what is commonly projected by the Western media. A person may even find that Islam provides the answers for all the questions and challenges in life.

May Allah guide us all to the truth.

---

[22] 'Heroes, Hero-Worship and the Heroic in History'